My Little Green Book

First steps in Bible reading

Christine Wright

Scripture Union, 207–209 Queensway, Bletchley, Milton Keynes, MK2 2EB
Internet: www.scriptureunion.org.uk

Scripture Union is an international Christian charity working with churches in more than 130 countries providing resources to bring the good news about Jesus Christ to children, young people and families – and to encourage them to develop spiritually through the Bible and prayer.

As well as a network of volunteers, staff and associates who run holidays, church-based events and school Christian groups, Scripture Union produces a wide range of publications and supports those who use the resources through training programmes.

First published 2003

ISBN 1 85999 696 5

Illustrations: Jenny Tulip at Beehive Illustration Agency
Cover and internal design: Mark Carpenter Design Consultants
Additional material: Val Mullally (pages 57, 63). The praise chant on page 12 is by Beth McLean and is taken from *Let's Sing and Shout!* © Scripture Union. The prayer by Christine Wright on page 45 was first published in *Bedtime Prayers*, Eagle Publishing © ADPS and is reprinted with permission.
Typesetting: Servis Filmsetting Ltd, Manchester
Printed and bound by Interprint Limited, Malta

What's in this book?

How to use this book

When children are small, before they can read, it can be hard to know how to introduce the Bible to them. The *Tiddlywinks Little Books* offer a simple and enjoyable way to do so. Each book introduces Bible stories and truths through the lives of young children today. As they explore and discover and learn about the Bible in their day-to-day lives, they share their discoveries with us.

There isn't a "right" way to use *Tiddlywinks Little Books*. If you'd like to read something every day, each numbered page gives you a story and a prayer idea. Alternatively, you could read several pages in one go for a longer story. *Little Books* do not tie you to a certain date: use them as often as suits you and your child. Young children enjoy hearing stories again and again so don't feel you have to keep moving on or can only read a section once. There are extra pages too with ideas for activities, rhymes and crafts, and things for the children to do themselves. There is also a page for you, as you seek to introduce ideas about God and the words of the Bible to the children in your care.

You might like to set aside a time for using the *Little Books*, perhaps at bedtime or while you have a meal together. Or keep the book handy so you can use it anytime – on a bus journey, at a pause in a day of busy playing or while you're waiting for a visitor to call.

Children in their early years are growing faster and learning more than at any other time in their lives – an ideal time to take their "First steps in Bible reading".

Meet Krista

Krista's almost four years old. She likes to have fun and find out about things. She wants to be helpful, but, somehow, she can't help knocking things over, spilling things and messing things up. She keeps trying though!

Some mornings, she goes to nursery and, once a week, she has fun at Tumble Tots. Her best friend is Lily, who lives next door. Krista's mum is expecting a baby soon. Mum, Dad and Krista talk about it lots. Krista is excited about "her baby" arriving.

One day Krista ran into the kitchen holding a book. "Look!" she shouted. Mum and Dad put down their cups of tea and looked. Krista opened her book and put it on the table.

"This new book's got everything in it," said Krista.

"What sort of things?" asked Mum.

"Birds and elephants and trees and wet things and people and a little baby like the one we're going to have soon," Krista said, turning the pages over very fast.

Dad looked to see.

"It's a story from the Bible about God's wonderful world," Dad told her.

"Can you read it to me?" Krista asked.

"Of course," said Mum and Dad. And they did – a little bit every day.

Turn the page to see what they read about.

"Hello! I'm Tiddly Ted.
Look for me as you share this book!"

Water, water everywhere!

Krista looked at her book. "There's nothing on this first page," she said. "Let's turn over and find another one."

"No," Dad explained, "it's a picture of what it was like before God created the world. That's why there isn't much to see. I'll read it to you." This is what he read:

"Long ago, before our wonderful world began, God was there. He started to make everything. At first, there was nothing growing, nothing living; just darkness and something amazing – water!"

Can you think of different places where you have seen water?

When God made water, he knew that all plants and animals would need it.

The Bible tells us all about it. Here's what the Bible says about God making water.

You take care of the earth and send rain to help the soil grow all kinds of crops...

You send showers of rain to soften the soil and help the plants sprout.

Pray

Thank you, God, for water!

Genesis 1:1–2; Psalm 65:9–10

Using water

Krista was in the bath. "Splish, splash, splish, splash!" she sang loudly as she whooshed the water over her legs.

"Be careful!" warned Mum, but it was too late. Water splashed out of the bath and fell on Mum's feet. Krista thought it was funny!

Later, as Mum tucked Krista into bed, she asked, "What have you done with water today? Can you remember?"

What do you think Krista might say?

Krista said, "I think water is fun." Mum added, "It's useful too, and not just for people."

Mum looked in the Bible. "God made water for animals and plants too. Let's see if you can guess what animals I'm reading about."

You can join in the game. Try to guess the noise Mum is making.

"Tweet, tweet," said Mum.

"Birds!" said Krista.

"Eey-aw!" said Mum.

"Donkeys!" shouted Krista.

"Moo!" said Mum.

"Cows!" yelled Krista.

Pray

Think of how you've used water today. Thank God for it.

Genesis 1:1–2; Psalm 104:10–16

Bright lights

Long ago, God made our wonderful world. At first, it was dark. Nothing was growing, nothing was living. And then God said, "Let there be light!"

Dazzling light appeared in the sky. The darkness was gone and the sea was speckled with gold. God made the sun which shines on us all through the day. He made the moon to give soft light at night. And he made a thousand, million stars to shine in the night sky.

How many stars can you count in this picture?

Krista likes this prayer of praise to God. It makes her think of sunny days and of night-time when the stars are twinkling and the moon is a bright curve in the sky.

Why don't you say it with her?

Sun and moon, and all you bright stars, come and offer praise . . .
Shout praises to the Lord!

Pray

Thank you, God, for lights in the day and lights in the night-time.

Genesis 1:3–5; Psalm 148:3,14

Night lights

Krista was playing with Dad in the garden. "It's getting dark," Dad said. "We won't be able to see what we're doing when the sun's gone down. We'd better go in."

Krista ran inside. The lights were already on in the house. She began to look for lights all around the house. Can you guess how many different lights she found?

At bedtime, when Krista looked out of the window, she saw other lights in the sky. The sun had disappeared, but she could see the moon and the stars. She bounced up and down on her bed, singing, "I like the dark; I like the light. I like the sun; I like the moon. I like the stars that shine so bright."

Then she looked again. "That's funny," she thought. "The moon isn't big and round tonight. It's like a banana. I wonder why?"

Pray

Can you make up a song like Krista's? Use it to say thank you to God for the light.

Genesis 1:16–19

See the sky!

Long ago, God made our wonderful world. At first, it was dark. Nothing was growing, nothing was living. Then God thought of something beautiful that he was going to make for all the plants and animals. It was something big, something blue, grey or white... It was the sky.

When the sun shone in the daytime, the sky was a brilliant light blue. At night, it was deepest, dark blue. In the day, fluffy clouds might be seen in the sky. At night, the stars twinkled in the sky. Look out of the window. What colour is the sky right now?

Can you colour this picture the same colour?

Krista has seen all these: blue sky, white clouds, grey sky, black clouds, red and orange sky early in the morning and sometimes in the evening. She likes the blue sky best of all. That means she can go out to play in the sunshine. Which do you like best?

Pray

I praise you, Lord God, with all my heart.
You spread out the sky above us.
With all my heart I praise you.

Genesis 1:6–8; Psalm 104:1–3

Looking at the sky

Krista's friend, Lily, had come to play. The girls ran out into the garden. Krista tripped over, but she wasn't hurt. She rolled over on the grass and lay on her back.

"Look, Lily!" she squealed. "The sky's like blue jelly with ice cream on top!"

Lily laughed. "God made the sky," she said.

"I know," replied Krista. "It's in my *God's wonderful world* book. The sky is for holding up the sun, and for holding up the stars and moon at night."

Do you think Krista is right? What do *you* think the sky is for?

One thing the sky does is to remind us how wonderful God is. Everything he made is good! One of the songs in the Bible says,

The heavens keep telling the wonders of God,
and the skies declare what he has done.

Pray

Hello, God!

When I look at the sky, I know how great you are!

Genesis 1:6–8; Psalm 19:1–2

God is great!

Here's a noisy praise chant to say together. Join in with **"God is great!"**

God made the sky.
God is great!
God made the sun.
God is great!
God made the moon.
God is great!
God made the stars.
God is great!
Wow! They're HUGE!
God is great!
Maybe we're too small to matter?
No! No! No! God loves us!
No! No! No! God loves us!

God is great.
God is great!
You're not too small to shout it out.
God is great!
You're not too small to sing about it.
God is great!
Come on world! Shout it out!
God is great!
Let your shout reach the sky!
God is great!

Land and sea

Long ago, God made our wonderful world. The sun shone in the beautiful blue sky; water sparkled in the sea. Then God made the land.

He made rocks, stones, sand, flat places, bumpy places, low valleys and tall mountains. He made seasides and beaches, fields and hills.

So now there was sea and land. But there was water on the land too. The rain drops fell on the hills. The drops collected together in pools and lakes. The pools and lakes got so big they spilt over and water ran down the hills as streams. The streams joined together to make bigger rivers. The rivers flowed through the land towards the sea. God had gathered the water into streams, rivers and lakes!

Point to the stones, flat place, river and hill in this picture.

Pray

Dear God, I love your wonderful world!

Genesis 1:9–10

Where are the mountains?

Krista was out shopping with Mum. She looked around and saw houses, flats and shops. She saw the road with cars and lorries rumbling along it.

"Why can't I see the mountains that God made?" she asked.

"Because," Mum explained, "this is a big town that people have built. All the buildings and roads were put on the land that God made. But it was built on a flat place. We'd have to go a long, long way to see any mountains."

On the way home, Mum took Krista to a travel agency. They looked at the shiny brochures and saw pictures of mountains, hills, beaches and the sea.

"Wow!" gasped Krista.

That evening, Krista made up her own prayer:

"Dear God, I like our town,
but I like the mountains and hills too. I like the sea and the beaches.
Thank you for making them."

Pray

Say Krista's prayer or make up your own.

Genesis 1:9–10

Growing things

Long ago, when God made our wonderful world, he said, "I want the land and sea to be filled with plants."

Beautiful plants began to grow. There were tall trees, waving grasses, lush water plants and seaweed. There were feathery ferns, colourful flowers, plants that grew fruit and nuts, and moss that grew in damp places.

The whole world was full of growing things that reached up to the sun. They grew roots deep into the ground to find water. They filled the land and grew up in fields and on hills. They even grew in rocky places. Some managed to grow in dry areas where it was very hot.

God was very pleased with what he had made.

What plants have you seen today? Have you seen trees, grass, flowers? What else?

Pray

Think about the plants that grow in your home or nearby. Thank God for all of them. Tell him what you like about the plants you see every day.

Genesis 1:11–13

Plants to eat

God made all sorts of plants. Plants to look at. Plants to eat. There's a song in the Bible that says,

I praise you, Lord God, with all my heart... You let the earth produce grass for cattle, plants for our food... and grain for our health.

Krista loves going to Lily's house because there is so much growing in her garden. One day, Lily and Krista found tiny apples growing on a small tree. Quickly, Krista picked them and ran to show her mum and Lily's mum.

"Oh no!" cried Krista's mum. "You should have left the apples on the tree to grow."

Krista felt bad.

Lily's mum said, "Never mind, Krista. You didn't know. I'll show you some other plants so that you can learn about how fruit grows." And that's what she did. "When the summer is over, Krista," she promised, "I'll pick a big, juicy apple just for you."

Pray

Thank God for the plants that we can eat. You could use the Bible words at the top of this page.

Psalm 104:1,14

How do apples grow?

Talk about these pictures. They show how apples grow on the branches of the apple tree.

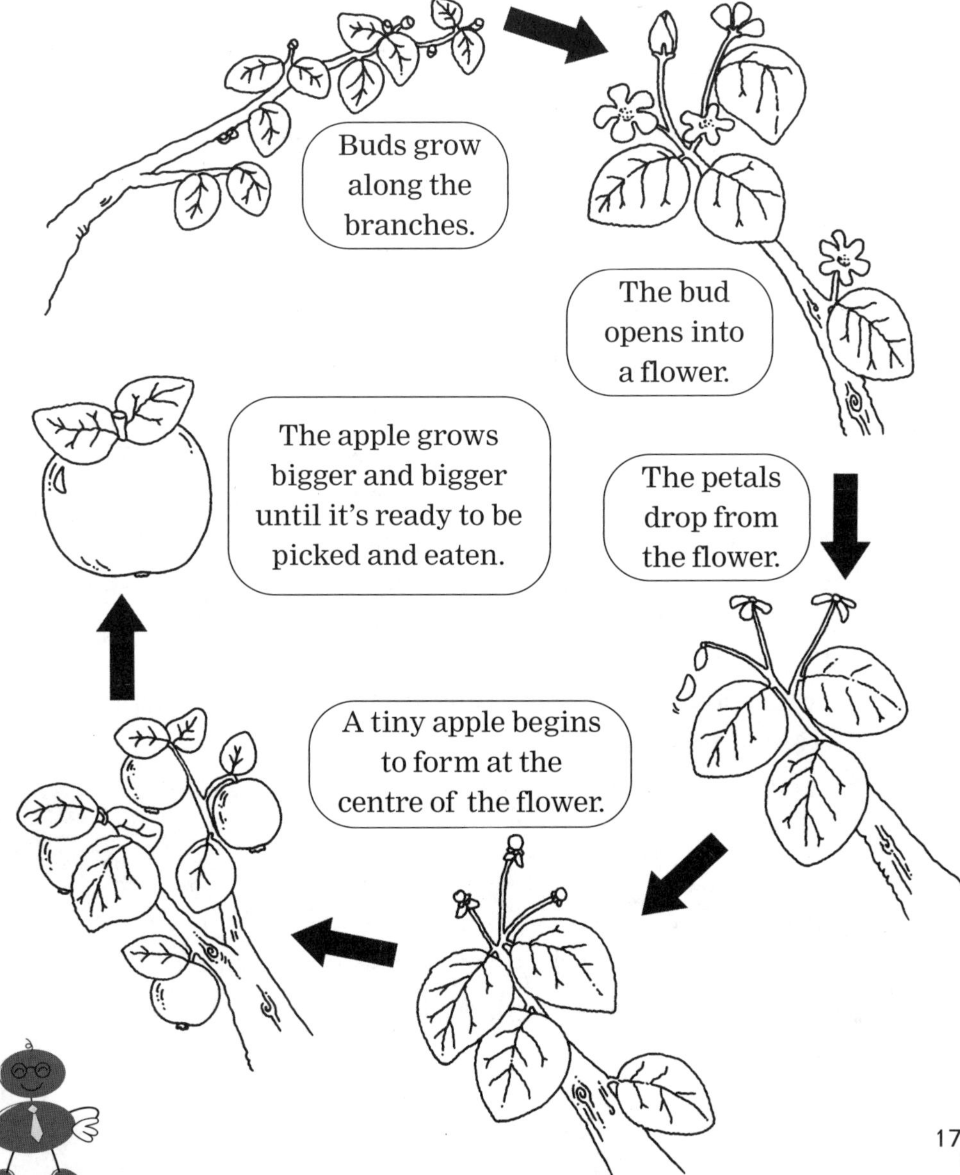

Wiggle and swim!

Have you ever seen fish swimming in a tank or a pool? Point to the right one when you hear about each fish.

A tiger barb is a quick, stripy fish.

A flounder is a flat fish that hides at the bottom of the sea.

A catfish has whiskers like a cat.

A hammerhead shark has a huge head.

When God made the world, he said, "I command the sea to be full of living creatures." So he made the giant sea creatures and all living things that swim in the sea. He told them to live everywhere in the sea, rivers and pools. And God was pleased with what he had done!

Can you pretend your hands are fish and make them swim in front of you?

Pray

Dear God, your world is wonderful. Even the fish are all different and all beautiful!

Genesis 1:20–23

All kinds of birds

Did you know that there are hundreds of different kinds of birds? Some are too big to fly and others are so small they look like bees. Some are dull grey or brown and others have brightly coloured feathers – red, yellow and blue. Penguins can dive under water to catch fish. Flamingos have long, long legs. And swifts can sleep while they are flying!

Have you seen any birds today? How big were they? What colour were they? Were they flying? God made every kind of bird. When he made the world he said, "I command birds to fly above the earth." And he told them to live everywhere on earth. God looked at what he had done, and thought it was good.

Can you pretend your hands are birds and make them fly above your head and in front of you?

Where do birds live? Read Psalm 104:16–17 to find some of the answers.

Pray

Dear God, help us to enjoy the birds we see every day, and to remember that they are your creatures.

Genesis 1:20–23

Big, bigger, biggest!

The page about big animals in her book, *God's wonderful world*, is one of Krista's favourites. When she looks at it, she likes to say this rhyme:

"Nobody fears
An elephant's ears.
Nobody likes
A porcupine's spikes.
Everyone laughs
At long, thin giraffes.
But nobody knows
Where the lonely whale goes."

Have you seen any big animals – really big animals? Here are pictures of parts of some big animals. Do you know which animals they belong to?

When God made the world, he wanted big creatures roaming around in the wild. So he made the elephant, the giraffe and the lion; the hippopotamus, the rhinoceros, and the blue whale that swims in the sea, the largest animal in the world. When he looked at what he had made, he was very pleased.

Can you use your face and hands to look like a tall giraffe? Like an elephant? Like a lion?

Pray

Thank God for all the big animals you can think of. He made every one of them, and he thinks they are really good!

Genesis 1:24–25

Mini-beasts

Krista has been watching the ants on the pavement outside her house. Whenever she goes out with Mum or Dad, she stops to see whether the ants are there. She often sees a line of tiny brown ants marching across the pavement like soldiers. Mum told her that the ants are looking for food to take back to their nests under the ground.

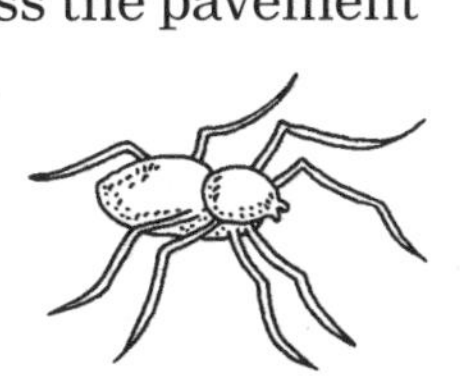

What is the smallest animal you can think of? Look around this page to see some of the tiniest animals that God created.

How many spiders can you find?
How many ants?
How many bees?

When God made the world, he wanted there to be tiny creatures. Some live in the soil. Some fly in the air. Some make honey from flowers. Some make beautiful webs.

God made every one of them. Then he looked at what he had done, and it was good.

Pray

Dear God, your world is wonderful! Thank you for spiders, for ants, for bees, for caterpillars and butterflies. We thank you!

Genesis 1:25

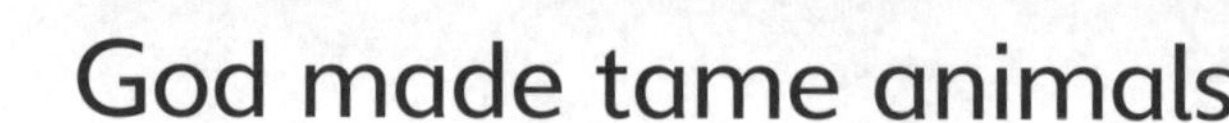

God made tame animals

Krista likes animals, but she can't have any pets at home. Animal hairs make Dad sneeze and sneeze! But when she's at nursery, she enjoys stroking the guinea pigs and helping to feed them. Guinea pig hairs don't make *her* sneeze!

Her very favourite animal is a dog called Buster. He belongs to Mr Chang. Krista always calls out, "Hello, Buster!" when she sees him. But she knows she mustn't pat him because Buster is taking Mr Chang down to the shops or the bus stop. Mr Chang can't see, and Buster has been trained to help Mr Chang get around safely.

God made some animals that can help people. Can you think of any others? Here are some clues:

Which animals give us milk to drink?

Which animals give us wool to make into clothes?

Which animals can we ride?

When God made the world, he created all kinds of animals and told people to care for them. Mr Chang feeds Buster, brushes his fur and makes sure he's well. Buster looks after Mr Chang too!

Pray

Dear God, thank you for animals that help us. Let us always look after them because they are all made by you.

God made reptiles

Did you know that some animals can't keep warm at night? They need the sun to heat up their blood. When it's dark, they can't move much until the sun comes out in the morning.

They are reptiles – tortoises, terrapins, crocodiles, snakes and lots of others. God made each one of them!

At nursery, Krista likes looking at the terrapins in the tank. They are like tiny tortoises and spend most of the day sitting on stones beside a pool of water. Krista knows that the terrapins have to live somewhere wet. They need to be kept warm too or they will die.

Here's a rhyme about a reptile. Can you guess which one?

More than twenty,
Teeth a-plenty.
Smiling, snapping,
Fishes trapping!
What is it?
A c_ _ _ _ _ _ _ _

"The reptile rhyme is about a crocodile."

God said, "I command the earth to give life to reptiles." And that's what happened. God made every one of them. Then he looked at what he had done and it was good.

Pray

Thank you, God, for all the strange and wonderful reptiles that you have made – smooth or scaly, slithering, sliding or so, so still.

Genesis 1:24–25

God's world: our world

Krista's dad was reading about God's wonderful world. He read:

"Long ago, when God made the world, it was full of beautiful and wonderful things. So God said, 'Let's make someone to enjoy the world with us.' That's why God made people to live in the wonderful world he had created."

"Wow!" shouted Krista, bouncing up and down. "God made people too. People like me and you and Mum and all my friends!"

"That's right," laughed Dad. "He made us to enjoy the world. And we do, don't we?"

"Yes, yes, YES!" laughed Krista.

Listen to this Bible song. Read it again, and then join in with "Come and praise the Lord!" The word "Lord" is another name for God, so this song is saying how great God is for making his wonderful world.

"Shout praises to the Lord! ... every man and every woman, young people and old, come, praise the Lord!"

Pray

God, you are great! Thank you for your wonderful world!

Genesis 1:27; Psalm 148:1,12

God gives people work to do

When God made his wonderful world, people were special. They were made to be clever enough to look after the world – everything in the sea, on the land and in the sky. God asked them to look after the animals and the plants and the sea and the land. What a lot of work!

Look in your Bible and find Genesis 1:28. Find out what God wanted people to look after – all the .... in the sea; all the .... in the sky; and every .... on earth.

There are three different creatures in this picture. Can you find all three?

What could you do this week to look after God's world?

Krista's idea for looking after the world is to help Dad fill a large flower pot with soil and compost. Then she can sow seeds and make flowers grow!

Pray

Dear God, there are lots of ways to look after your world – growing plants, caring for animals, looking after other people, keeping things tidy. Please help us to do our share.

Genesis 1:27–30

God gives people food

One day, at the supermarket, Mum spotted a pile of ripe bananas. "I know," she told Krista, "we'll buy some and I'll show you how to make honey-baked bananas." Krista loves bananas and honey, so she thought that was a great idea. Look on the next page to see how Mum cooked the bananas.

What are your favourite foods?

Did you know that most of our food is grown by farmers? They grow fruit, vegetables and other crops. They look after animals which give us food. Perhaps your family grows food too! Most food is sent to shops, where we buy it.

When God made the world, he told people, "I have given all kinds of fruit and grain for you to eat."

God knew that people need food to make them strong and to help them grow. That's why he has given us so many good things to eat.

What food can you see in this picture?

Pray

When I'm hungry, God, I really like to eat...................

(Finish this prayer with your own ideas.)

Honey-baked bananas

Krista and Mum have been busy in the kitchen, making a delicious pudding.

If you want to try making honey-baked bananas, here's what to do.

You will need:

4 ripe bananas

20 g of soft brown sugar

1 lemon

20 ml of honey

4 large squares of foil (big enough to wrap a banana)

What to do:

Grate the lemon rind and squeeze all the juice into a bowl.
(A grown-up will need to do this.)

Peel the bananas and put each one on to a square of foil.

Sprinkle sugar, lemon rind and lemon juice over the bananas.

Drizzle 5 ml of honey over each one.

Fold and seal the foil around the banana to make a packet.

(A grown-up must do the final stages.)

Place the packets in a hot oven or under a hot grill.

Leave the packets for about ten minutes.

Open the packets carefully and serve the bananas in their foil containers.

Eat and enjoy!

! Remember to wash your hands before you do any cooking.
Honey isn't good for very young children: don't give this to anyone who is under one year old.

God makes new people

When God made people, he told them to have a lot of children so that there would always be enough people to look after his world.

Krista had nearly finished reading her book about God's wonderful world. The last picture showed lots and lots of people. They had different skin and hair colours and wore different kinds of clothes. There were children and old people... and babies.

Can you find the baby in this picture?

Krista knew that very soon, she would have a baby brother or sister. She told everyone she met about it!

"Will God make our new baby?" she asked Mum, who was sitting beside her.

"Yes," Mum replied. "He already has. The baby is living inside my tummy, growing bigger and stronger until it's the right time to be born."

Talk about any babies you know. What are their names? How old are they? Is there a baby in your family? Do any of

Pray

Dear God, thank you for every new person that's born into your world. Each one belongs to you.

Genesis 1:28

God gives us babies

Krista was very excited. "Not many more days now," said Mum, "and our new baby will be born!"

Whenever they went out, Krista looked out for babies in buggies and car seats. "Not long now!" she whispered to herself.

There's a Bible story about Elizabeth and Zechariah who prayed that they'd have a baby. They were old now and still hadn't had a child. They had prayed for a long, long time, asking God to give them a family. One day, God sent an angel to tell Zechariah that God had heard their prayers. God gave them a wonderful promise. Can you guess what it was? Read these words from the Bible to find out:

"Don't be afraid, Zechariah! God has heard your prayers. Your wife Elizabeth will have a son, and you must name him John. His birth will make you very happy, and many people will be glad."

Elizabeth and Zechariah were so surprised! They were happy that they would soon have what they'd always wanted – a baby of their own.

Pray

Loving God, thank you for new babies. They make their families happy!

Luke 1:13–14

A baby is born

One day, Krista's mum and dad had to go to hospital. Krista went to Lily's house next door. Just after lunch, Dad arrived. He had a big smile. "Krista, our new baby has been born. It's a girl. We're going to call her Molly."

Krista gave him a big hug. "Can I go and see her?" she asked. Dad took her straight away. Krista thought her new sister was beautiful. "Hello, Molly," she whispered.

In the Bible story, when Zechariah and Elizabeth's baby was born, all their friends and family came to see the baby and find out his name. Some of them thought he should be called Zechariah, like his father. But Elizabeth said, "No, his name had already been chosen!" They called the baby the name that the angel had said he must have. Can you remember what it was? If not, read Luke 1:13–14.

Pray

All babies are very special. Think of babies you know and their names. Ask God to bless them all.

Luke 1:13–14, 57–60

God gives us children

Babies can't even put their own socks on, but you probably can. You might need help with buttons and zips, but when you're seven, you'll be able to dress all on your own. There will still be lots of things, though, that you'll need a grown-up to help you with.

How old are you? Do you know a baby who isn't one yet? Do you know a child who is seven?

That's how old Joash was when he became king! Kings and queens and other important people are usually grown-ups, but Joash was a child. He didn't know how to do things properly and he needed someone to help him.

A priest called Jehoiada taught Joash how to be king and how to do what was right. Because he'd learnt to do what was right when he was a child, Joash obeyed God all his life.

Pray

I'm learning lots of things too, God. Help me to remember to do what's right and obey you. Amen.

2 Kings 12:2

Children can obey God

Baby Molly is too small to have friends. But Krista has lots of children to play with. She has Lily who lives next door. Sometimes she plays with Lily's brothers and sisters too, but it's more fun with Lily because she's the same age as Krista. At Tumble Tots, Krista likes all the children, but especially Reese who is her special friend.

What do you and your friends like to do together?

When Krista, Lily and Reese play well together and are kind to each other, they are doing what God wants. He loves them to play happily.

King Joash learnt to obey God when he was a child. He told everyone to give money to repair the temple where people went to worship God. He knew it was right to make the temple as beautiful as possible. That was his way of doing what God wanted.

Pray

Help us, loving God, to do what you want every day.

2 Kings 12:4–5

God gives us friends

When Krista plays at Lily's house, Lily shares her toys with Krista. When Lily plays at Krista's house, Krista shares with Lily. They are good friends.

The Bible has a story about two friends, David and Jonathan. Jonathan was very important – the king's son. David was just a young man who looked after sheep. But when they met, they liked each other and became best friends. Jonathan said to David, "Don't go back and look after sheep. Stay here with me and live in the king's house."

Because Jonathan was the king's son, he had plenty of fine clothes. David didn't have much at all, so Jonathan shared what he had. Look at this picture. What did Jonathan give to David?

Pray

Thanks for friends who share and friends who care!

1 Samuel 18:1–5

Friendly games

Here are some easy games to play with a friend. Ask a grown-up to help you.

Row your boat

What to do:
Sit facing each other on the floor.
Move forward until you can hold hands.
Pull your friend gently towards you.
Let your friend pull you gently.
Keep doing this while you sing:

Row, row, row your boat,
Gently down the stream,
Merrily, merrily, merrily, merrily.
Life is but a dream!

Back to back

Sit on the floor with your back resting against your friend's back. How long can you sit like this before someone wriggles?

Friends who care

At Tumble Tots one day, Reese slipped over and bumped his head. Krista saw what had happened and ran to fetch Reese's dad. Krista was so upset that Reese was hurt that *she* began to cry! But Reese soon felt better and joined in the fun again. Krista was so pleased that he was all right.

In the Bible story, Jonathan and David were friends. Jonathan cared what happened to David. When David was in danger, Jonathan did what he could to help.

"The king wants to hurt me," David told Jonathan. At first Jonathan couldn't believe it. The king was Jonathan's dad.

"Jonathan, I swear it's true!" David said.

Then Jonathan said, "Tell me how I can help you and I'll do it." Jonathan managed to get David away to a safe place. What a good friend!

Pray

Help me, dear God, to be a good friend.
Thank you for friends who care for me.

1 Samuel 20:1–9

Krista is famous!

There was a lovely photograph in the newspaper. It was of Krista holding baby Molly. It even had their names underneath. “You’re famous!” laughed Dad.

“Why?” asked Krista. Dad told her that lots of people would look at the photo and know that she had a new baby sister.

Krista told Lily that she was famous, but Lily said, “Not as famous as the Queen. Everyone knows about her.”

There is a Bible story about a queen called Esther. She was chosen to be queen because she was so beautiful. The king loved her so much that he gave everyone in the land a day off their work and gave her expensive presents.

Esther heard that her cousin, Mordecai, was very unhappy. She sent her servant to find out why. He said that God’s people, the Jews, were in terrible danger. Esther thought about this. If she helped her people, it would mean that she was in danger too. But she knew she must be brave.

“I will help,” she said.

Pray

Think of famous people you know about. Ask God to help them in their work.

Esther 2:17–20

Queen Esther helps others

Sometimes, famous people are able to help ordinary people and this is a Bible story about a time when this happened.

Long ago, Queen Esther heard that her people, the Jews, were in danger. She knew that the king could stop anything dreadful happening, but she was not allowed to go to see the king unless he called for her. What could she do?

She went to the king. It was very brave as the king could have been angry. But he was pleased to see her and asked if he could help her.

"Your Majesty," she replied, "if you really care for me and want to help, save me and my people." The king gave orders to make sure that the Jews were not harmed. Esther was glad that she had been able to help her people – all because she was the queen.

Pray

Thank you, loving God, for famous people who do all they can to help others.

Esther 7:1–4

Busy with the baby

Sometimes, Krista's mum and dad were very busy looking after Molly. At first, Krista got very cross because she wanted Mum and Dad to look at what she was doing.

"Don't get upset," Mum said. "Molly is only a baby. There are lots of things that she can't do for herself. Would you like to help me? You can help look after Molly too."

Can you think of some of the things that Molly needed help with?

There was once a baby called Samuel. His mother, Hannah, had been asking God for a baby for a long time. She made a special promise to God. She said, "Please let me have a son. I will let him help you for as long as he lives." She was very glad when Samuel was born and she looked after him when he was too small to do things for himself. But Hannah remembered her promise to God. One day soon she would take Samuel to work for God. She was sure this was a good thing to do and that Samuel would be happy serving God all his life.

Pray

Think about the people who look after you. How do they help you? Say thank you to God for people who care about you.

1 Samuel 1:10–11

Caring for each other

When Samuel was old enough, it was time for him to go and live with a man called Eli. This is what his mother, Hannah, had promised God. She knew that Eli would look after him and would teach him how to serve God.

Hannah said, "I asked God to give me a child. God gave me what I asked for. This is my child, Samuel. Now, Samuel will come and work for God."

Eli did care for Samuel. He looked after him and he told him all about God. But Eli was quite old. He couldn't run about and sometimes he was very tired. So then Samuel had to do things for him. Samuel cared for Eli too!

What can you do to show you care for other people – at home, out shopping or at your friend's house? Which of these pictures shows children who care for each other?

Pray

Hello, God! Thank you for people who care for me. Thank you that I can care for others too.

1 Samuel 1:26–28

Showing and doing

When Krista went to Tumble Tots, the teacher, Avril, showed her how to go head over heels. Then she helped Krista practise until she could do it too! Krista had learnt to do something by watching Avril and then trying it herself.

One evening, Jesus showed his friends something new! He took a towel and a bowl of water and washed their feet. His friends had seen people washing feet before – it happened all the time in those days because the dust and dirt from the roads made everyone's feet dirty and sticky. But they'd never seen anyone as important as Jesus doing it.

Jesus was teaching his friends not to argue about who was the most clever or the strongest. Instead, they should love each other and care for each other. He didn't just tell them what to do. They learned by watching Jesus doing what they should do for each other.

Pray

Dear Jesus, help our family to show how much we love each other.

John 13:5

Love each other

It was time for Jesus to go away. Soon his friends wouldn't see him any more. So Jesus wanted to teach them what they must do.

"Love each other," he said. "That's what I want you to do. Then everyone will know that you're my friends. Everyone will know that you love me."

Here's a short rhyme to learn to help you remember what Jesus taught his friends.

Don't argue.
Do not fight.
All that whining
Isn't right.

This is what
We can do:
Love like Jesus
Taught us to.

At Lily's house one day, Krista tried on Lily's pink ballet shoes. Lily was angry. "Give them back!" she yelled.

At first, Krista shouted, "No!"

Lily began to cry and her mum came to see what was wrong. She said to Krista, "Those pink shoes are very special. Lily is afraid you'll spoil them." Lily's mum showed Krista other shoes to dress up in. "Well done, Krista," she said, as Krista took the pink shoes off. "You've been a good friend to Lily."

Pray

Hello, Jesus! Please teach us how to love each other and help us when it's hard. Amen.

John 13:34–35

Ten men meet Jesus

"Ouch!" cried Krista. A wasp was stinging her arm. Krista called Mum to come and help. In no time at all, Mum had put some cream on her arm and was giving her a cuddle. For a few days, Krista had a red blotch on her skin, but she soon forgot all about it.

Jesus met some men with sore skin, but they didn't think they'd *ever* get better!

The ten men all had sore skin. Other people wouldn't go near them in case they got sore skin too. The men saw Jesus and called out, "Jesus, please help us!"

Jesus heard them and came over. He said, "Go and see the priest. He'll tell you that you're well now." As they went, they saw that they *were* well! Their skin was no longer sore or itchy. They were so happy! Jesus had healed them.

Count the men in this picture. Are there ten?

Pray

Do you know anyone who is not well?
If so, ask Jesus to help make them well.
If not, thank Jesus that you are well!

Luke 17:11–14

Saying "thank you"

Jesus healed ten men who had itchy, sore skin. Some of them went on their way. They were glad to be healed, but they didn't think about Jesus any more.

Look at this picture. How many men came back to Jesus?

One man came back, shouting praises to God. He bowed down at Jesus' feet and looked up into Jesus' smiling face. He said, "Thank you, Jesus. You healed me."

Jesus looked around. "Weren't there ten men who were healed?" he asked. "And only one has come back to thank me."

Then he looked again at the man at his feet. Jesus was so pleased that he'd said thank you. "You are really, truly well. Get up and go home now," he told the man.

Pray

What would you like to thank Jesus for today? Remember, he's pleased when we say "thank you"!

Luke 17:15–19

Talking to God

Krista's family are learning to talk to God. "What can we talk to God about?" her mum asked. Krista wasn't sure, so Dad said, "We could say thank you."

"For Molly!" shouted Krista. "Our own new baby!" Then she remembered that Molly woke everyone up in the night by crying very loudly. "Only sometimes she makes us cross," Krista added.

Mum suggested, "So we could say sorry to God for being cross with Molly."

Dad added, "We could ask God to help us be more patient. Molly's still only a little baby."

Jesus talked to God too. He told his friends that prayers don't need to be long. "Your Father God knows what you need, so just ask," he said. "You can pray on your own and God will hear you. You don't have to stand outside and shout. Just speak quietly. God understands."

Pray

Today, say a short prayer to our Father God! You could say "thank you" or "sorry". God understands!

Matthew 6:7–8

A bedtime prayer

Learning to pray

Krista's family knows a special prayer. It's called "The Lord's Prayer". Krista thinks some of the words are too hard, but she likes trying to say it with Mum and Dad. Molly is too small to say the prayer. She makes baby noises. Krista says, "That's how she talks to God!"

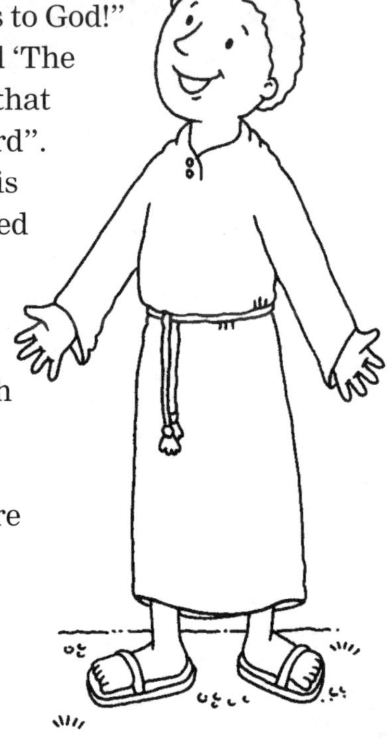

Krista asked, "Why is it called 'The Lord's Prayer'?" Mum explained that sometimes we call Jesus "The Lord". And Dad said that Jesus taught his friends this prayer when he wanted them to know how to talk to God. "So we could call it 'The Jesus Prayer' too," he told Krista.

One day, Jesus wanted to teach his friends how to talk to God. He started the prayer by calling God "Our Father". When we pray, we're talking to God who loves us very much. God loves us even more than good fathers and mothers love their children.

Pray

Do you know "The Lord's Prayer"? If you do, say it together. Or say your own prayer beginning "Our Father..."

Matthew 6:9–15

The farmer and the seeds

The flowers in Krista's flowerpot were growing well, but she still needed to look after them. Every day, she watered them and pulled out any weeds that might stop them growing properly. Krista thinks growing plants is fun, but hard work!

Sometimes, big crowds of people gathered around Jesus. He taught them lots of things about God, but they didn't always listen carefully. So one day he told a story about a farmer who sowed lots of seed in his field, but it didn't all grow very well.

This is a picture of the farmer's field. Point to the right places when you hear where the farmer sowed the seed. Use the pictures on the next page too.

Some seed fell on the path.

Some fell where big weeds and thorns grew.

Some fell on rocky ground.
Some fell on good soil.
Which seed do you think would grow best?

Pray

Dear God, thank you for plants that grow so we can have food to eat and flowers to enjoy.

Luke 8:5–8

Seed and plants

Jesus told a story about a farmer sowing seed.

Point to the right places when you hear how the seed grew in different places. Use the pictures on page 47 too.

The seed that fell on the path didn't last long. Birds came and ate it and people trod on it as they walked along the path. The seed that fell on the rocks and stones quickly became small plants, but didn't have enough water and soon died away. The seed that fell among big weeds grew, but the plants were soon choked and couldn't grow any more. But the seed that fell on the good soil, grew quickly and kept on growing until the plants were tall and strong. The farmer was pleased to see how the plants grew in the good soil.

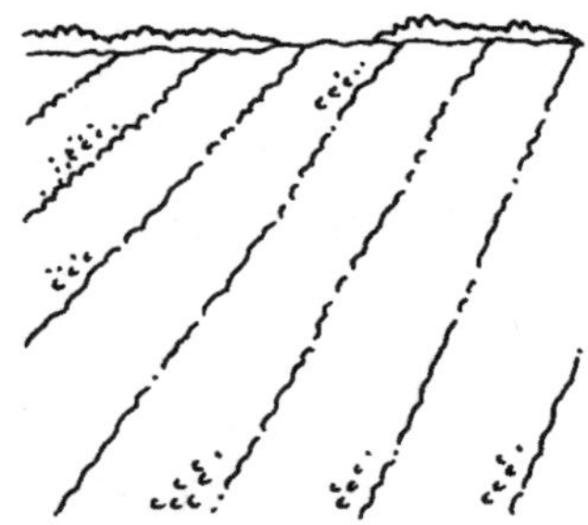

Draw strong, tall plants in the picture of the good soil.

Pray

Jesus, thank you for telling stories.

Reading God's book

Although Krista can't read yet, she loves books. Every week, she comes home from the library with lots of books. Most of them have colourful pictures and some have stories.

There's a special book in Krista's house too. It's a Bible. It doesn't have many pictures and Krista can't read it, but Mum and Dad show her where her favourite stories are. Do you have a Bible? Find it and hold it open.

When Jesus was a boy, he didn't go to the sort of schools we have. His father taught him at home and showed him how to work with wood and be a carpenter. The sort of "church" he went to was different too. It was a building called the "synagogue" and Jesus went there to learn about the Bible. Jesus knew it was God's book. When he grew older, he could read God's book himself!

Here's a game you can play – ask a grown-up to find the name "Jesus" somewhere in the Bible. See if you can find the word again on the same page. Get someone to help if you find it hard.

Pray

Dear Jesus, I'm glad you read the Bible too!

Luke 2:52

Reading the Bible

Before you start, why not find your Bible and have it ready?

If you go to church, you'll probably hear someone reading the Bible out loud. Jesus went to the synagogue (which was a bit like church) every week. One day, he was asked to be the person who reads the Bible out loud.

Jesus loved reading from the Bible. He opened God's book and began. This is what he read out: "The Holy Spirit is with me because God has chosen me. I've come to bring good news to those who are poor, to let people go free, to make blind people see and to help anyone who is suffering."

When he'd finished, he sat down and said, "These words were written long ago, but today they are coming true. God is about to start something wonderful. He's sending me to tell everyone good news."

Wow! Everyone in the synagogue was amazed!

Pray

Dear God, thank you that your book, the Bible, shows us how wonderful Jesus is.

Luke 4:18

Happy birthday, Krista!

It was Krista's birthday. She was four years old! In the morning, she had presents to open – there was even one from Molly! In the afternoon, all her friends came for a party and then, when it was nearly time for everyone to go home, she saw her birthday cake. On the top were lighted candles – all ready for her to blow out.

Can you draw the right number of candles on the cake?

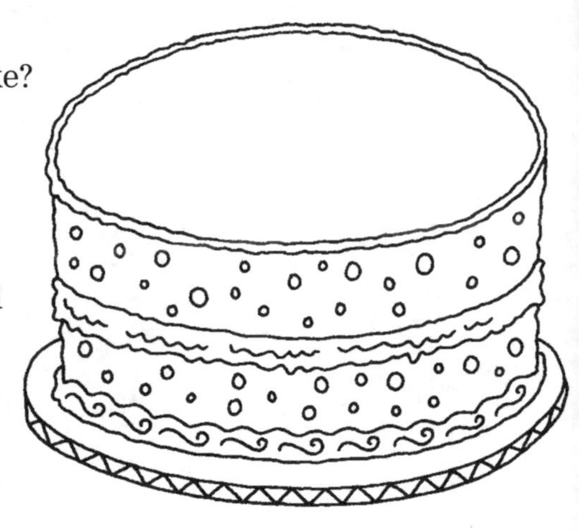

That evening Krista felt very happy. She asked Mum and Dad to tell her the happiest story they knew. They found the Bible and told her a story about Jesus. "But it starts very sadly," they told her. "Jesus' friends thought he was dead, but they were in for a big surprise!"

You can hear about the story in Matthew 28:1–10. There are lots of surprises in the story – an earthquake, an angel and, best of all, Jesus' friends found that he was alive again!

Pray

Dear Jesus, the story of you coming back to life is the happiest story ever. Thank you for happy times like ...

(Finish this prayer by telling God about your own happy times.)

The happiest story

Jesus' friends thought he was dead, but they were in for a big surprise! Two women, both called Mary, went to the place where Jesus' body was. They were very sad. They thought they'd never see Jesus again.

Suddenly, there was a loud noise and the earth shook. When the two Marys looked up, they saw an angel who said, "Don't be afraid. Jesus isn't dead any more. He's come back to life, just as he said he would. Now hurry back and tell all his friends that Jesus is alive."

The two Marys felt scared and excited. As they hurried home, they met Jesus himself. How wonderful! Jesus told them not to be afraid. He really was alive!

Krista was very happy when she heard this story. "I liked it when Jesus was alive again," she said sleepily.

Pray

Dear God, you know how I feel. When I'm sad, please take care of me and make me happy again soon.

Matthew 28:1–10

A cross king

Jesus told a story about a king who got very angry. The king said to his servant, "You owe me a lot of money. It's time to give it back."

The servant said, "I can't pay. Give me more time."

The king felt sorry for him. "I'll let you off. You don't have to pay me anything."

Later, the servant saw a friend. "You owe me some money," he said. "Give it back."

The friend said, "I can't. Give me more time."

But the king's servant said, "If you can't pay now, you'll go to prison until you can."

When the king heard this, he was very, very cross. "I was fair to you," he told his servant, "but you were unfair to your friend. Now you must pay back all the money you owed to me!"

Try to count how many coins the man owed the king. Can you count them all?

Pray

Dear Jesus, please help us to forgive our friends and family when they make us cross. Help us to make things all right again.

Matthew 18:21–35

Krista gets cross

Nothing was going right for Krista and she was getting very cross. To start with, Molly was crying, so Krista asked if she could go and play with Lily. The two girls went into the garden, but it began to rain. Krista wanted to play with Lily's toys, but Lily wouldn't let her. "I want to go home!" she told Lily's mum.

Back home, Krista wanted a cuddle, but Molly was still crying and Mum was talking to someone on the phone. What do you think Krista did next? What do you do when you get cross?

Krista knew it was wrong, but she tipped all the CDs out of the rack! That made Mum cross too. But later, Mum said, "I'm sorry you had a bad day."

They cuddled up together and Krista said, "Sorry I was cross."

"I understand," Mum told her. "And so does God. We can't help getting cross sometimes. It's all right now, though."

Dear God, we are sorry when we get cross, especially when we do something to hurt other people. Please forgive us.

James 1:19–20

Krista is sad

Krista's family were getting ready to go and visit Nanny. Krista packed her favourite teddy and some pictures she'd drawn. Then the phone rang. It was Nanny. She had a bad cold and didn't want Molly and Krista to catch it. They couldn't go after all.

Krista unpacked her bag feeling very sad. Mum said she could post Nanny the pictures, but it didn't stop Krista feeling sad.

That evening, Krista asked for a story about someone who was sad. Mum found a Bible story about a man called Nehemiah. He wanted to be back home, in Jerusalem, but he couldn't go.

Nehemiah had heard news that something bad had happened in Jerusalem. You can find out what it was by reading Nehemiah 1:3. The walls were.................... and the gates were.................

That made Nehemiah feel very sad. But what could he do? Read on to find out!

Pray

Dear Father God, when we are sad, you know all about it. Thank you for understanding our sadness.

City walls

This song tells you more about Nehemiah. Sing it to the tune of "London Bridge is falling down".

City walls are broken down,
Broken down, broken down.
City walls are broken down.
Call Nehemiah!

Nehemiah cried and prayed,
Cried and prayed, cried and
prayed.
Nehemiah cried and prayed
"Lord, please help me!"

God will tell you what to do,
What to do, what to do.
God will tell you what to do,
Nehemiah!

Build those walls back up again,
Up again, up again.
Build those walls back up again,
Nehemiah!

Lots of people helped to build,
Helped to build, helped to
build.
Lots of people helped to build.
The wall round the city.

Nehemiah prayed to God,
Prayed to God, prayed to God.
Nehemiah prayed to God
Till the wall was finished!

Nehemiah is sad

Nehemiah was very sad when he heard that Jerusalem had been destroyed, so he asked God to help him. Nehemiah's job was to look after the king. One day, the king saw that Nehemiah looked sad and asked him why. Nehemiah explained, "I feel sad because the city where I used to live is in ruins. The walls are broken down and the big gates have been burnt."

"Do you want me to help you?" asked the king.

Nehemiah replied, "Please send me back to Jerusalem, so that I can build the city again."

The king allowed Nehemiah to go home. In Jerusalem, Nehemiah rode on a donkey all around the city. He saw the broken down walls and the burnt gates. He was still sad, but he decided to build the walls and gates up again!

Pray

Think of times when you have felt sad. Remember that God knows and understands when we are sad. Say thank you to him.

Krista feels shy

Have you ever felt shy and scared? Krista doesn't often feel shy, but one day she had to go and meet her new childminder. Mum was going back to work, so Krista and Molly had someone new to look after them during the day. The childminder's name was Alison.

When they arrived, Krista hid behind Mum. She didn't know what Alison would be like! But soon Krista started talking to Alison. She was very nice!

That evening she told Dad about Alison and Mum said, "You were a bit shy at first, weren't you?"

Krista nodded.

Dad said to Krista, "I'll tell you a Bible story about someone who was shy and scared. His name was Gideon. God wanted him to do something new – chase away the army that was in his land. It would mean he'd have to be very brave, but Gideon didn't want to! In the end, though, he learnt to trust God and he found people to help him chase the army away."

Pray

Dear God, I feel shy and scared sometimes. You know how I feel. Help me to be brave.

Judges 6:14–15

Gideon is scared

Gideon was hiding. There were enemy soldiers all around. He didn't want them to find him, but God knew where he was!

God told him, "You're a brave soldier and I'm going to help you chase away the enemy."

Gideon said, "No, I'm from a very weak family and I'm the weakest person in my family."

God replied, "You can rescue your people from the enemy because I'm going to help you."

And that's what happened. Scared Gideon became strong Gideon because God was with him. He chased the enemy soldiers away with just a few other men.

Look at the picture to see what Gideon's men used to make a big, scary noise.

It's good to know that God can help us when we don't feel brave. No matter how shy or scared we are, God is with us and helps us to be strong.

Pray

Dear God, I'm glad you can make scared people strong and brave.

Judges 6:14–16; 7:19–22

Busy Krista

Krista was busy. Mum took her shopping to buy some new shoes. Then she went swimming with Lily and her mum. After lunch, she went to a farm with all the children from Tumble Tots. And after that she helped Mum with the shopping at the supermarket.

That evening, she said, "I'm tired! Is it bedtime yet?"

Mum laughed. "You've been so busy today. No wonder you're tired. Before you settle down, I'll tell you a Bible story about a man who was very busy."

This is the story she told:

"Hezekiah was always busy because he was a king – a good king who tried to do what God wanted. He made sure that he always obeyed God. He wouldn't let other kings come into his country and make his people do wrong things. He made sure that none of his people had their food or homes taken away by their enemies. There was a lot for Hezekiah to do!"

Pray

Hello, Jesus! I love being busy. Thank you for being with me today when........................

(Finish the prayer with things you have done today.)

2 Kings 18:5–6

Busy Hezekiah

"The Assyrians are coming!" people shouted. "They'll take away our houses and steal all the food we're growing in the fields."

King Hezekiah told all his people, "Don't be afraid. Even though there are enemies all around us, God will help us and we'll be safe."

But the Assyrians told the people, "Your king, Hezekiah, has been busy telling you that you'll be safe. Don't listen to him. Your God can't help you."

When Hezekiah heard what the Assyrians were saying, he prayed. There was so much to do, but he knew he needed God's help.

"Please help us," he prayed. "The Assyrians are about to attack us."

God did help. He sent an angel to defeat the Assyrian army. Soon the rest of the Assyrians had all gone home and Hezekiah's people were safe in their homes again.

Krista liked hearing about Hezekiah. She said, "I'm busy too, aren't I?"

Mum and Dad nodded. "But not too busy to enjoy stories from the Bible!" they said.

Krista agreed!

Pray

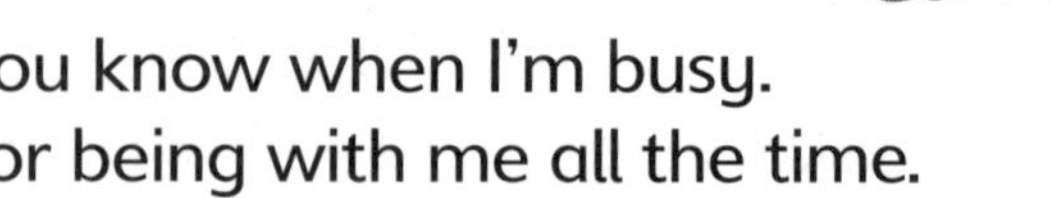

Dear God, you know when I'm busy. Thank you for being with me all the time.

2 Kings 18:5–7,28–30; 19:14,19,32–34

First steps in praying with young children

You may have heard the story of the young child who came home after his first week at school and announced, "Our headteacher's name is Harold!"

"How do you know?" his mother enquired.

"Because this morning he stood up and prayed, 'Our Father, who art in heaven. Harold is my name'."

What is obvious to adults isn't always obvious to children, who have such limited life experience. Jesus certainly gave his adult followers the Lord's Prayer as a model – but we need to "feed our lambs." After all, young lambs do not have the same diet as sheep!

This is particularly true of prayer. Children just chat to God. They are not weighed down with ponderous vocabulary and heavy theological issues.

"Jesus is my friend and I can talk to him, wherever I am," could well be summed up as the young child's theology of prayer.

Children pray naturally and easily, when set the example. Just rely on the KISS principle – Keep It Short and Simple! Create an environment where children learn to delight in being with God spontaneously, rather than long devotional sessions, which are beyond the young child's level of concentration. (Psalm 100:2)

Very young children are likely to bring their "pleases" but as they grow a little older they will learn to say "thank you", especially if we model this to them, through prayer and sharing our own experiences of answered prayer. Even saying grace at meals sets this example. Children are usually over four years old before they begin to understand that we need to pray "sorry" prayers – to tell Jesus that we are sad when we have done something wrong.

The important thing is, let prayer be a natural part of daily life in each child's life, right from the time of conception. And you may find that to KISS helps your own prayer life too!